ADVENTURES
in
MEAL PLANNING

Your guide to easily planning meals
for your busy life

JENNI WARD

Founder of The Gingered Whisk

Cover illustration and interior design by Grace + Vine Studios
Edited by Holly Norian, Fancy Fox

Independently published by Jennifer Ward

ISBN: 978-0-578-82791-9

Printed in the United States of America

www.thegingeredwhisk.com

Table of Contents

MEET YOUR GUIDE 5

WHY YOU SHOULD BE MEAL PLANNING 6

4 SIMPLE STEPS 8

STEP 1: MAKE A FAVORITE MEAL ROTATION LIST 9

    MEALS BY PROTEIN 10

    MEALS BY TECHNIQUE 16

    MEALS BY SEASON 22

    MEALS BY CUISINE 26

STEP 2: PLAN YOUR FREQUENCY 36

STEP 3: LOOK AT YOUR WEEKLY SCHEDULE 37

    THEME NIGHTS 38

STEP 4: FILL IN YOUR MENU! 40

    TRUSTED RESOURCES FOR NEW RECIPES 42

WEEKLY MEAL PLANNING CALENDARS 44

SEASONAL REFRESH 70

WEEKLY MEAL PLANNING CALENDARS 74

SEASONAL REFRESH 100

WEEKLY MEAL PLANNING CALENDARS 104

SEASONAL REFRESH 130

WEEKLY MEAL PLANNING CALENDARS 134

SEASONAL REFLECTION 160

CONGRATULATIONS 162

Hello.

I'm Jenni, and I'll be your meal planning guide. I live in Iowa with my husband and our three young girls, and I fully understand what it's like to have a full and busy life. Amidst rushing home from an activity or just trying to survive the chaotic hours between school and bedtime, you need the dinner process to be easy.

But I firmly believe that easy meals don't have to be boring just because you are short on time! I LOVE food, and I love GOOD food. Even with full and busy days filled with young kids, I refuse to "settle" with boring food because it's easy.

That's why I am a huge fan of everyone having a custom meal plan that actually helps you not only survive the night, but thrive in it.

I want to help you break out of your daily dinnertime struggle—from the preparation of the meal, to getting the kids to actually try a small bite, to discovering new recipes that aren't boring or bland.

I want you to feel excitement about your food, and I want you to be proud of your family's dinner time together.

Learning how to meal plan is the key to sticking to your grocery budget, your diet plan, and keeping your weeks and days running more smoothly! Meal planning looks different for everyone, and this guide will help you create a plan that is perfect for your family! My goal is to make this process effective and easy for you, whatever that might look like.

Why You Should Be Meal Planning

The whole point of meal planning is to create a system that simplifies your life. Here are my favorite 8 ways that a custom meal plan can change your life.

1. Not have to think about it the rest of the week (which we could all totally use, right?).

2. Not getting stuck in the monotonous routine of the same meals each week (tacos, tacos, tacos).

3. Not continuously going out to eat because you don't have anything to eat at home.

4. Cuts down on screaming temper tantrums when it's 4:30 and your children are dying of starvation.

5. Spending too much time at the grocery store because you don't know what to buy.

6. Reduces impulse purchases (goodbye, Double Stuffed Oreos!)

7. Helps you stick to a budget because you are buying only the things you need, and not buying things you don't have a plan for.

8. Reduces the amount of trips you take to the store because you forgot items.

Why You Need Your Own Meal Plan and Not a Premade One

Creating your own meal plan that fits your life and your family's needs is really the only way to go.

Premade meal plans seem great on the surface, but they don't take into account **your** schedule, **your** tastes and preferences, **your** dietary needs, **your** budget, etc.

Creating your own meal plan is the only way to ensure that your dinners are actually attainable in the time you have, that your family will enjoy them, and that they will fit your lifestyle.

How to Make Meal Planning Work for YOU in 4 Simple Steps

Right now, you may be thinking that meal planning is a lot of work, it's going to take a long time. You may be feeling anxious about it. Not to worry.

We are going to break this down into super simple steps that will help you to create a system that easily adjusts to your life, so you can spend less time planning meals (and less time at the grocery store, less time managing food tantrums...you read that list, right?) and more time doing the things you would rather be doing!

There are four simple steps that we are going to use, and doing them in this order, consistently, will help you create a meal plan that fits your family's needs, and hopefully makes dinnertime more fun!

1. List out your favorite tried-and-true recipes that your family loves.

2. Decide how often you want to plan your meals and go grocery shopping.

3. Consider your family's unique weekly schedule for this season.

4. Build your menu and shopping list.

Make a Favorite Meal Rotation List

The following pages are for you to write down your family's favorite meals. As many as you can think of!

By creating a master list of your favorite family-loved meals, it's easier to rotate through all the things you love—instead of only being able to think about, say...tacos. This turns meal planning into a plug and play situation, which makes the whole thing super quick!

You are also going to categorize all of your favorite recipes by type of protein, by kind of recipe (casserole, soup, crock pot meal), by season, and by cuisine type. As you find new recipes your family loves, add them to the list, too!

Again, this is to help you rotate through your meals in a simple way but to still give you variety in your menu. It may seem a little repetitive, but that is ok!

Hint

It is ok to list the same recipe under multiple headings. Organize your recipes so that it makes the most sense to **you**.

Favorite Egg Recipes

RECIPE	WHERE TO FIND
_____	_____
_____	_____
_____	_____
_____	_____
_____	_____
_____	_____
_____	_____
_____	_____
_____	_____
_____	_____
_____	_____
_____	_____
_____	_____
_____	_____
_____	_____
_____	_____
_____	_____
_____	_____
_____	_____
_____	_____

Favorite Beef Recipes

RECIPE	WHERE TO FIND

Favorite Chicken & Turkey Recipes

RECIPE	WHERE TO FIND

Favorite Meatless Recipes

RECIPE	WHERE TO FIND

Favorite Pork Recipes

RECIPE	WHERE TO FIND

Favorite Seafood Recipes

RECIPE	WHERE TO FIND

Favorite Slow Cooker Recipes

RECIPE	WHERE TO FIND

Favorite Super Quick Recipes

RECIPE	WHERE TO FIND

Favorite 30 Minute Recipes

RECIPE	WHERE TO FIND

Favorite Grilling Recipes

RECIPE	WHERE TO FIND

Favorite One Pan Recipes

RECIPE	WHERE TO FIND

Favorite Soup Recipes

RECIPE	WHERE TO FIND

Favorite Spring Recipes

RECIPE	WHERE TO FIND

Favorite Summer Recipes

RECIPE	WHERE TO FIND

Favorite Fall Recipes

RECIPE	WHERE TO FIND

Favorite Winter Recipes

RECIPE	WHERE TO FIND

African Recipes

RECIPE	WHERE TO FIND

American Recipes

RECIPE	WHERE TO FIND

Asian Recipes

RECIPE	WHERE TO FIND

European Recipes

RECIPE	WHERE TO FIND

Indian Recipes

RECIPE	WHERE TO FIND

Latin American Recipes

RECIPE	WHERE TO FIND

Mediterranean Recipes

RECIPE	WHERE TO FIND

Middle Eastern Recipes

RECIPE	WHERE TO FIND

Nordic Recipes

RECIPE	WHERE TO FIND

Other Recipes

RECIPE	WHERE TO FIND

2 *Plan Your Frequency*

Take a moment and think about how often you want to plan your meals and go grocery shopping. Every week? Every two weeks? Once a month?

If you only want to shop once a month, you totally can! But you will also need to get creative when it comes to milk, bread and produce (hint: you can freeze them!). It just depends on what works best for your family and your schedule.

You can also decide to plan for two weeks or a whole month at one time, but still go grocery shopping every week. It's completely up to you.

How often do you go to the grocery store now?

_____

_____

How often do you want to go to the grocery store?

_____

_____

What can you do to change from what you are currently doing to what you want to do?

_____

_____

How many days do you need to meal plan for at a time?

_____

_____

Look at Your Weekly Schedule

Think about your average weekly schedule for this season. What events do you have going on you need to remember? Think about meetings, lessons, after school activities, etc. List out what your typical schedule looks like.

day	*typical schedule*
MONDAY	
TUESDAY	
WEDNESDAY	
THURSDAY	
FRIDAY	
SATURDAY	
SUNDAY	

Theme Nights

Using theme nights is an excellent way to make your meal planning EVEN quicker, because you know exactly what type of recipe you are looking for when planning. It's part of that "plug and play" thing we are working towards, and this is just one more step that helps your meal planning take a little less brain power.

You can do this several ways. You can schedule by cuisine type—like Meatball Monday or Taco Tuesday. You can also schedule by technique type—like Slow Cooker Night or Super Quick Night. You can also switch it up and use it multiple ways! Theme nights can be fun, functional, or both.

Examples of how to use theme nights functionally:

I know that our girls have horseback riding lessons that end at 6:00pm on Thursday evenings, so on Thursdays I always schedule a slow cooker meal so that dinner is waiting for us when we get home. Thursdays = Slow Cooker Night

I know that my husband typically has late meetings on Wednesdays, and I will be making dinner without him at home, so I always pick a quick 15 minute meal on those nights. Wednesdays = 15 Minute Dinners

Theme Night Examples

Feel free to write in your own theme night ideas, too!

By Weeknight:

- Slow Sunday
- Spaghetti Sunday
- SOUP-er Sunday
- Something New Sunday
- Meatless Monday
- Meatball Monday
- Taco Tuesday
- Waffle Wednesday
- Waste Not Wednesday (leftover night)
- World Traveler Wednesday
- Fish Friday
- Stir-FRY-Day

General Ideas

- Pasta Night
- Taco Night
- International Night
- Soup and Sandwich Night
- Slow Cooker Night
- Sheet Pan Night
- Casserole Night
- Seafood Night
- Grilling Night
- Leftover Night
- Breakfast for Dinner Night
- Kid's Choice Night
- Take Out/Eat Out Night
- Movie Matchup Night
- Pizza Night
- Sandwich Night
- Baked Potato Night
- Bar Night (Taco Bar, Waffle Bar, Salad Bar)
- Salad Night

What theme night(s) do you want to incorporate into your meal plan this season?
Circle or highlight them above.

4 *Fill In Your Menu!*

The following pages contain your Weekly Meal Planning Calendars for the next year! Every 13 weeks, you will find Seasonal Refresh pages for you to make any necessary adjustments, for both changes in weather and changes in your schedule. If you're starting your adventure in meal planning in the middle of a season, simply jump ahead to the Seasonal Refresh page when it's time to shake things up.

Ok, let's get started! Look back at Step 2: Plan Your Frequency to determine how many weekly meal plans you want to complete in one sitting. Then follow the instructions below to fill in your menu(s).

1. Start with breakfast (because it's the easiest). It's ok to have the same breakfasts a few times a week. You don't have to reinvent the wheel!

2. Fill in your dinners, pulling from your Favorite Meal Rotation List and keeping your schedule, the weather, and your theme nights in mind. Plug and go!

3. Then write in your lunches. Think about leftovers you may have.

4. Lastly, fill in any snacks you are going to need.

More Awesome Planning Tips

 Adding a variety of meat, different kinds of meals (salads, casseroles, crock pots, etc.) will keep your menu feeling fresh.

 Try to use ingredients for more than one meal. Cook a giant pork roast early in the week, and use it for multiple meals throughout the week. If you buy a big tub of ricotta cheese but only need half for a particular recipe, how can you add the remainder to your menu?

 As you place meals in your menu, double check ingredients you already have on hand, and write the items you will need on your grocery list. Creating your shopping list as you make your meal plan saves time, helps use what you already have, and saves you from forgetting anything you need at the store.

 Plan for eating out. I mean, really. If you have a doctors appointment at 10:45am and swimming lessons at 1:00pm, you are not going home to cook lunch. Nope, you are headed straight to Chick-Fil-A, my friend, and don't even pretend you're not. Just go ahead and add it to your plan!

 Add one new recipe every week or two, if you feel like trying new things. Not only does this give you an excuse to try out the 16,000 recipes you have collected online and torn out of magazines, but it helps you to add new favorites to your list and expand your family's repertoire!

A note on new recipes:

Adding new recipes to your meal plan is fun and exciting. It's a great way to discover new cuisines, explore new ingredients, and change up your normal. But adding new recipes to your weekly meal plan willy nilly can actually cause more undue stress than you thought.

Cooking a recipe for the first time takes longer—you need to stop and check the recipe more often, and you are slower preparing it. When scheduling a NEW recipe, make sure you do it on an easy schedule day with plenty of time, so you don't feel rushed.

Trusted Resources for New Recipes

Knowing WHERE to find new recipes you want to try is important.

Pinterest and Google can be overwhelming, especially since it's hard to know if the search results are well-written recipes.

Use this space to list out your trusted cookbooks, magazines, websites, and blogs that you love, so you know where to look when you want to try a new recipe.

MAGAZINES	*COOKBOOKS*	*WEBSITES & BLOGS*
		thegingeredwhisk.com

52 Weeks

of

Meal Planning Calendars

Week of _____

What's going on this week? Is there anything in your schedule that will affect what
time you eat or how you prepare meals?

_____

_____

What is the weather this week? Write the forecast at the top of your Meal Plan, and make
any notes here of things that might affect how you cook (using the oven, grill, etc.) or what
kind of meals you want to make.

_____

_____

What theme nights do you want to include this week?

_____

_____

Is there any meal prep you can do ahead of time to make your meals easier?

_____

_____

Cross off any meals that you do NOT need to make this week.

Meal Plan

	MON	TUES	WED	THURS	FRI	SAT	SUN
WEATHER							
BREAKFAST							
SNACK							
LUNCH							
SNACK							
DINNER (SCHEDULE/THEME/ RECIPE SOURCE)							
DESSERT							

Week of _____

What's going on this week? Is there anything in your schedule that will affect what time you eat or how you prepare meals?

_____

_____

What is the weather this week? Write the forecast at the top of your Meal Plan, and make any notes here of things that might affect how you cook (using the oven, grill, etc.) or what kind of meals you want to make.

_____

_____

What theme nights do you want to include this week?

_____

_____

Is there any meal prep you can do ahead of time to make your meals easier?

_____

_____

Cross off any meals that you do NOT need to make this week.

Meal Plan

	MON	TUES	WED	THURS	FRI	SAT	SUN
WEATHER							
BREAKFAST							
SNACK							
LUNCH							
SNACK							
DINNER (SCHEDULE/THEME/ RECIPE SOURCE)							
DESSERT							

Week of _____

What's going on this week? Is there anything in your schedule that will affect what time you eat or how you prepare meals?

_____

_____

What is the weather this week? Write the forecast at the top of your Meal Plan, and make any notes here of things that might affect how you cook (using the oven, grill, etc.) or what kind of meals you want to make.

_____

_____

What theme nights do you want to include this week?

_____

_____

Is there any meal prep you can do ahead of time to make your meals easier?

_____

_____

Cross off any meals that you do NOT need to make this week.

Meal Plan

	MON	TUES	WED	THURS	FRI	SAT	SUN
WEATHER							
BREAKFAST							
SNACK							
LUNCH							
SNACK							
DINNER (CHEDULE/THEME/ RECIPE SOURCE)							
DESSERT							

Week of _____

What's going on this week? Is there anything in your schedule that will affect what time you eat or how you prepare meals?

_____

_____

What is the weather this week? Write the forecast at the top of your Meal Plan, and make any notes here of things that might affect how you cook (using the oven, grill, etc.) or what kind of meals you want to make.

_____

_____

What theme nights do you want to include this week?

_____

_____

Is there any meal prep you can do ahead of time to make your meals easier?

_____

_____

Cross off any meals that you do NOT need to make this week.

Meal Plan

	MON	TUES	WED	THURS	FRI	SAT	SUN
WEATHER							
BREAKFAST							
SNACK							
LUNCH							
SNACK							
DINNER (SCHEDULE/THEME/ RECIPE SOURCE)							
DESSERT							

Week of _____

What's going on this week? Is there anything in your schedule that will affect what time you eat or how you prepare meals?

_____

_____

What is the weather this week? Write the forecast at the top of your Meal Plan, and make any notes here of things that might affect how you cook (using the oven, grill, etc.) or what kind of meals you want to make.

_____

_____

What theme nights do you want to include this week?

_____

_____

Is there any meal prep you can do ahead of time to make your meals easier?

_____

_____

Cross off any meals that you do NOT need to make this week.

Meal Plan

	MON	TUES	WED	THURS	FRI	SAT	SUN
WEATHER							
BREAKFAST							
SNACK							
LUNCH							
SNACK							
DINNER (SCHEDULE/THEME/ RECIPE SOURCE)							
DESSERT							

Week of _____

What's going on this week? Is there anything in your schedule that will affect what time you eat or how you prepare meals?

_____

_____

What is the weather this week? Write the forecast at the top of your Meal Plan, and make any notes here of things that might affect how you cook (using the oven, grill, etc.) or what kind of meals you want to make.

_____

_____

What theme nights do you want to include this week?

_____

_____

Is there any meal prep you can do ahead of time to make your meals easier?

_____

_____

Cross off any meals that you do NOT need to make this week.

Meal Plan

	MON	TUES	WED	THURS	FRI	SAT	SUN
WEATHER							
BREAKFAST							
SNACK							
LUNCH							
SNACK							
DINNER (SCHEDULE/THEME/ RECIPE SOURCE)							
DESSERT							

Week of _____

What's going on this week? Is there anything in your schedule that will affect what time you eat or how you prepare meals?

_____

_____

What is the weather this week? Write the forecast at the top of your Meal Plan, and make any notes here of things that might affect how you cook (using the oven, grill, etc.) or what kind of meals you want to make.

_____

_____

What theme nights do you want to include this week?

_____

_____

Is there any meal prep you can do ahead of time to make your meals easier?

_____

_____

Cross off any meals that you do NOT need to make this week.

Meal Plan

	MON	TUES	WED	THURS	FRI	SAT	SUN
WEATHER							
BREAKFAST							
SNACK							
LUNCH							
SNACK							
DINNER (CHEDULE/THEME/ RECIPE SOURCE)							
DESSERT							

Week of _____

What's going on this week? Is there anything in your schedule that will affect what time you eat or how you prepare meals?

_____

_____

What is the weather this week? Write the forecast at the top of your Meal Plan, and make any notes here of things that might affect how you cook (using the oven, grill, etc.) or what kind of meals you want to make.

_____

_____

What theme nights do you want to include this week?

_____

_____

Is there any meal prep you can do ahead of time to make your meals easier?

_____

_____

Cross off any meals that you do NOT need to make this week.

Meal Plan

	MON	TUES	WED	THURS	FRI	SAT	SUN
WEATHER							
BREAKFAST							
SNACK							
LUNCH							
SNACK							
DINNER (SCHEDULE/THEME/ RECIPE SOURCE)							
DESSERT							

Week of _____

What's going on this week? Is there anything in your schedule that will affect what time you eat or how you prepare meals?

_____

_____

What is the weather this week? Write the forecast at the top of your Meal Plan, and make any notes here of things that might affect how you cook (using the oven, grill, etc.) or what kind of meals you want to make.

_____

_____

What theme nights do you want to include this week?

_____

_____

Is there any meal prep you can do ahead of time to make your meals easier?

_____

_____

Cross off any meals that you do NOT need to make this week.

Meal Plan

	MON	TUES	WED	THURS	FRI	SAT	SUN
WEATHER							
BREAKFAST							
SNACK							
LUNCH							
SNACK							
DINNER (SCHEDULE/THEME/ RECIPE SOURCE)							
DESSERT							

Week of _____

What's going on this week? Is there anything in your schedule that will affect what time you eat or how you prepare meals?

_____

_____

What is the weather this week? Write the forecast at the top of your Meal Plan, and make any notes here of things that might affect how you cook (using the oven, grill, etc.) or what kind of meals you want to make.

_____

_____

What theme nights do you want to include this week?

_____

_____

Is there any meal prep you can do ahead of time to make your meals easier?

_____

_____

Cross off any meals that you do NOT need to make this week.

Meal Plan

	MON	TUES	WED	THURS	FRI	SAT	SUN
WEATHER							
BREAKFAST							
SNACK							
LUNCH							
SNACK							
DINNER (SCHEDULE/THEME/ RECIPE SOURCE)							
DESSERT							

Week of _____

What's going on this week? Is there anything in your schedule that will affect what time you eat or how you prepare meals?

_____

_____

What is the weather this week? Write the forecast at the top of your Meal Plan, and make any notes here of things that might affect how you cook (using the oven, grill, etc.) or what kind of meals you want to make.

_____

_____

What theme nights do you want to include this week?

_____

_____

Is there any meal prep you can do ahead of time to make your meals easier?

_____

_____

Cross off any meals that you do NOT need to make this week.

Meal Plan

	MON	TUES	WED	THURS	FRI	SAT	SUN
WEATHER							
BREAKFAST							
SNACK							
LUNCH							
SNACK							
DINNER (CHEDULE/THEME/ RECIPE SOURCE)							
DESSERT							

Week of _____

What's going on this week? Is there anything in your schedule that will affect what time you eat or how you prepare meals?

_____

_____

What is the weather this week? Write the forecast at the top of your Meal Plan, and make any notes here of things that might affect how you cook (using the oven, grill, etc.) or what kind of meals you want to make.

_____

_____

What theme nights do you want to include this week?

_____

_____

Is there any meal prep you can do ahead of time to make your meals easier?

_____

_____

Cross off any meals that you do NOT need to make this week.

Meal Plan

	MON	TUES	WED	THURS	FRI	SAT	SUN
WEATHER							
BREAKFAST							
SNACK							
LUNCH							
SNACK							
DINNER (SCHEDULE/THEME/ RECIPE SOURCE)							
DESSERT							

Week of _____

What's going on this week? Is there anything in your schedule that will affect what time you eat or how you prepare meals?

_____

_____

What is the weather this week? Write the forecast at the top of your Meal Plan, and make any notes here of things that might affect how you cook (using the oven, grill, etc.) or what kind of meals you want to make.

_____

_____

What theme nights do you want to include this week?

_____

_____

Is there any meal prep you can do ahead of time to make your meals easier?

_____

_____

Cross off any meals that you do NOT need to make this week.

Meal Plan

	MON	TUES	WED	THURS	FRI	SAT	SUN
WEATHER							
BREAKFAST							
SNACK							
LUNCH							
SNACK							
DINNER (SCHEDULE/THEME/ RECIPE SOURCE)							
DESSERT							

Seasonal Refresh

Welcome to a new season!

With every change of season comes a change in weather, schedules, and day-to-day activity. Use these pages to reflect on and refresh your meal plan so that it continues to work for you and fit your life.

Think back over the past 3 months.

How did your meal planning fit into your life over the past few months?

_____

_____

What worked really well for you that you want to keep doing?

_____

_____

What didn't work so well that you would like to change?

_____

_____

How many meals did you plan for during each planning session? Do you want to keep that number the same or change it?

_____

_____

How often did you go grocery shopping? Do you want to keep that frequency the same or change it?

_____

_____

What are your family's favorite recipes lately? What have you been trying and loving? (Make sure these are on your Favorite Meal Rotation List.)

_____

_____

Did you discover any new cookbooks, magazines, or blogs that you love? Add these to your resources list!

_____

_____

Now think ahead to the next 3 months...

Look at Your Weekly Schedule

Think about your average weekly schedule for this season. What events do you have going on you need to remember? Think about meetings, lessons, after school activities, etc. List out what your typical schedule looks like.

day	*typical schedule*
MONDAY	
TUESDAY	
WEDNESDAY	
THURSDAY	
FRIDAY	
SATURDAY	
SUNDAY	

How is the weather changing? How will the change affect the way you want to cook and eat? (For example, in Winter you may want more soups; during Summer you may want to grill more often, etc.)

_____

_____

Is there anything new you know you want to try? A new recipe, cuisine, or ingredient? How can you add this to your plan?

_____

_____

Do you want to add or swap out any theme nights?

_____

_____

Week of _____

What's going on this week? Is there anything in your schedule that will affect what time you eat or how you prepare meals?

_____

_____

What is the weather this week? Write the forecast at the top of your Meal Plan, and make any notes here of things that might affect how you cook (using the oven, grill, etc.) or what kind of meals you want to make.

_____

_____

What theme nights do you want to include this week?

_____

_____

Is there any meal prep you can do ahead of time to make your meals easier?

_____

_____

Cross off any meals that you do NOT need to make this week.

Meal Plan

	MON	TUES	WED	THURS	FRI	SAT	SUN
WEATHER							
BREAKFAST							
SNACK							
LUNCH							
SNACK							
DINNER (SCHEDULE/THEME/ RECIPE SOURCE)							
DESSERT							

Week of _____

What's going on this week? Is there anything in your schedule that will affect what time you eat or how you prepare meals?

_____

_____

What is the weather this week? Write the forecast at the top of your Meal Plan, and make any notes here of things that might affect how you cook (using the oven, grill, etc.) or what kind of meals you want to make.

_____

_____

What theme nights do you want to include this week?

_____

_____

Is there any meal prep you can do ahead of time to make your meals easier?

_____

_____

Cross off any meals that you do NOT need to make this week.

Meal Plan

	MON	TUES	WED	THURS	FRI	SAT	SUN
WEATHER							
BREAKFAST							
SNACK							
LUNCH							
SNACK							
DINNER (CHEDULE/THEME/ RECIPE SOURCE)							
DESSERT							

Week of _____

What's going on this week? Is there anything in your schedule that will affect what time you eat or how you prepare meals?

_____

_____

What is the weather this week? Write the forecast at the top of your Meal Plan, and make any notes here of things that might affect how you cook (using the oven, grill, etc.) or what kind of meals you want to make.

_____

_____

What theme nights do you want to include this week?

_____

_____

Is there any meal prep you can do ahead of time to make your meals easier?

_____

_____

Cross off any meals that you do NOT need to make this week.

Meal Plan

	MON	TUES	WED	THURS	FRI	SAT	SUN
WEATHER							
BREAKFAST							
SNACK							
LUNCH							
SNACK							
DINNER (SCHEDULE/THEME/ RECIPE SOURCE)							
DESSERT							

Week of _____

What's going on this week? Is there anything in your schedule that will affect what time you eat or how you prepare meals?

_____

_____

What is the weather this week? Write the forecast at the top of your Meal Plan, and make any notes here of things that might affect how you cook (using the oven, grill, etc.) or what kind of meals you want to make.

_____

_____

What theme nights do you want to include this week?

_____

_____

Is there any meal prep you can do ahead of time to make your meals easier?

_____

_____

Cross off any meals that you do NOT need to make this week.

Meal Plan

	MON	TUES	WED	THURS	FRI	SAT	SUN
WEATHER							
BREAKFAST							
SNACK							
LUNCH							
SNACK							
DINNER (SCHEDULE/THEME/ RECIPE SOURCE)							
DESSERT							

Week of _____

What's going on this week? Is there anything in your schedule that will affect what time you eat or how you prepare meals?

_____

_____

What is the weather this week? Write the forecast at the top of your Meal Plan, and make any notes here of things that might affect how you cook (using the oven, grill, etc.) or what kind of meals you want to make.

_____

_____

What theme nights do you want to include this week?

_____

_____

Is there any meal prep you can do ahead of time to make your meals easier?

_____

_____

Cross off any meals that you do NOT need to make this week.

Meal Plan

	MON	TUES	WED	THURS	FRI	SAT	SUN
WEATHER							
BREAKFAST							
SNACK							
LUNCH							
SNACK							
DINNER (SCHEDULE/THEME/ RECIPE SOURCE)							
DESSERT							

Week of _____

What's going on this week? Is there anything in your schedule that will affect what time you eat or how you prepare meals?

_____

_____

What is the weather this week? Write the forecast at the top of your Meal Plan, and make any notes here of things that might affect how you cook (using the oven, grill, etc.) or what kind of meals you want to make.

_____

_____

What theme nights do you want to include this week?

_____

_____

Is there any meal prep you can do ahead of time to make your meals easier?

_____

_____

Cross off any meals that you do NOT need to make this week.

Meal Plan

	MON	TUES	WED	THURS	FRI	SAT	SUN
WEATHER							
BREAKFAST							
SNACK							
LUNCH							
SNACK							
DINNER (SCHEDULE/THEME/ RECIPE SOURCE)							
DESSERT							

Week of _____

What's going on this week? Is there anything in your schedule that will affect what time you eat or how you prepare meals?

_____

_____

What is the weather this week? Write the forecast at the top of your Meal Plan, and make any notes here of things that might affect how you cook (using the oven, grill, etc.) or what kind of meals you want to make.

_____

_____

What theme nights do you want to include this week?

_____

_____

Is there any meal prep you can do ahead of time to make your meals easier?

_____

_____

Cross off any meals that you do NOT need to make this week.

Meal Plan

	MON	TUES	WED	THURS	FRI	SAT	SUN
WEATHER							
BREAKFAST							
SNACK							
LUNCH							
SNACK							
DINNER (SCHEDULE/THEME/ RECIPE SOURCE)							
DESSERT							

Week of _____

What's going on this week? Is there anything in your schedule that will affect what time you eat or how you prepare meals?

_____

_____

What is the weather this week? Write the forecast at the top of your Meal Plan, and make any notes here of things that might affect how you cook (using the oven, grill, etc.) or what kind of meals you want to make.

_____

_____

What theme nights do you want to include this week?

_____

_____

Is there any meal prep you can do ahead of time to make your meals easier?

_____

_____

Cross off any meals that you do NOT need to make this week.

Meal Plan

	MON	TUES	WED	THURS	FRI	SAT	SUN
WEATHER							
BREAKFAST							
SNACK							
LUNCH							
SNACK							
DINNER (CHEDULE/THEME/ RECIPE SOURCE)							
DESSERT							

Week of _____

What's going on this week? Is there anything in your schedule that will affect what time you eat or how you prepare meals?

_____

_____

What is the weather this week? Write the forecast at the top of your Meal Plan, and make any notes here of things that might affect how you cook (using the oven, grill, etc.) or what kind of meals you want to make.

_____

_____

What theme nights do you want to include this week?

_____

_____

Is there any meal prep you can do ahead of time to make your meals easier?

_____

_____

Cross off any meals that you do NOT need to make this week.

Meal Plan

	MON	TUES	WED	THURS	FRI	SAT	SUN
WEATHER							
BREAKFAST							
SNACK							
LUNCH							
SNACK							
DINNER (SCHEDULE/THEME/ RECIPE SOURCE)							
DESSERT							

Week of _____

What's going on this week? Is there anything in your schedule that will affect what time you eat or how you prepare meals?

_____

_____

What is the weather this week? Write the forecast at the top of your Meal Plan, and make any notes here of things that might affect how you cook (using the oven, grill, etc.) or what kind of meals you want to make.

_____

_____

What theme nights do you want to include this week?

_____

_____

Is there any meal prep you can do ahead of time to make your meals easier?

_____

_____

Cross off any meals that you do NOT need to make this week.

Meal Plan

	MON	TUES	WED	THURS	FRI	SAT	SUN
WEATHER							
BREAKFAST							
SNACK							
LUNCH							
SNACK							
DINNER (CHEDULE/THEME/ RECIPE SOURCE)							
DESSERT							

Week of _____

What's going on this week? Is there anything in your schedule that will affect what time you eat or how you prepare meals?

_____

_____

What is the weather this week? Write the forecast at the top of your Meal Plan, and make any notes here of things that might affect how you cook (using the oven, grill, etc.) or what kind of meals you want to make.

_____

_____

What theme nights do you want to include this week?

_____

_____

Is there any meal prep you can do ahead of time to make your meals easier?

_____

_____

Cross off any meals that you do NOT need to make this week.

Meal Plan

	MON	TUES	WED	THURS	FRI	SAT	SUN
WEATHER							
BREAKFAST							
SNACK							
LUNCH							
SNACK							
DINNER (CHEDULE/THEME/ RECIPE SOURCE)							
DESSERT							

Week of _____

What's going on this week? Is there anything in your schedule that will affect what time you eat or how you prepare meals?

_____

_____

What is the weather this week? Write the forecast at the top of your Meal Plan, and make any notes here of things that might affect how you cook (using the oven, grill, etc.) or what kind of meals you want to make.

_____

_____

What theme nights do you want to include this week?

_____

_____

Is there any meal prep you can do ahead of time to make your meals easier?

_____

_____

Cross off any meals that you do NOT need to make this week.

Meal Plan

	MON	TUES	WED	THURS	FRI	SAT	SUN
WEATHER							
BREAKFAST							
SNACK							
LUNCH							
SNACK							
DINNER (SCHEDULE/THEME/ RECIPE SOURCE)							
DESSERT							

Week of _____

What's going on this week? Is there anything in your schedule that will affect what time you eat or how you prepare meals?

_____

_____

What is the weather this week? Write the forecast at the top of your Meal Plan, and make any notes here of things that might affect how you cook (using the oven, grill, etc.) or what kind of meals you want to make.

_____

_____

What theme nights do you want to include this week?

_____

_____

Is there any meal prep you can do ahead of time to make your meals easier?

_____

_____

Cross off any meals that you do NOT need to make this week.

Meal Plan

	MON	TUES	WED	THURS	FRI	SAT	SUN
WEATHER							
BREAKFAST							
SNACK							
LUNCH							
SNACK							
DINNER (SCHEDULE/THEME/ RECIPE SOURCE)							
DESSERT							

Seasonal Refresh

Welcome to a new season!

With every change of season comes a change in weather, schedules, and day-to-day activity. Use these pages to reflect on and refresh your meal plan so that it continues to work for you and fit your life.

Think back over the past 3 months.

How did your meal planning fit into your life over the past few months?

_____

_____

What worked really well for you that you want to keep doing?

_____

_____

What didn't work so well that you would like to change?

_____

_____

How many meals did you plan for during each planning session? Do you want to keep that number the same or change it?

_____

_____

How often did you go grocery shopping? Do you want to keep that frequency the same or change it?

_____

_____

What are your family's favorite recipes lately? What have you been trying and loving? (Make sure these are on your Favorite Meal Rotation List.)

_____

_____

Did you discover any new cookbooks, magazines, or blogs that you love? Add these to your resources list!

_____

_____

Now think ahead to the next 3 months...

Look at Your Weekly Schedule

Think about your average weekly schedule for this season. What events do you have going on you need to remember? Think about meetings, lessons, after school activities, etc. List out what your typical schedule looks like.

day	*typical schedule*
MONDAY	
TUESDAY	
WEDNESDAY	
THURSDAY	
FRIDAY	
SATURDAY	
SUNDAY	

How is the weather changing? How will the change affect the way you want to cook and eat? (For example, in Winter you may want more soups; during Summer you may want to grill more often, etc.)

_____

_____

Is there anything new you know you want to try? A new recipe, cuisine, or ingredient? How can you add this to your plan?

_____

_____

Do you want to add or swap out any theme nights?

_____

_____

Week of _____

What's going on this week? Is there anything in your schedule that will affect what time you eat or how you prepare meals?

_____

_____

What is the weather this week? Write the forecast at the top of your Meal Plan, and make any notes here of things that might affect how you cook (using the oven, grill, etc.) or what kind of meals you want to make.

_____

_____

What theme nights do you want to include this week?

_____

_____

Is there any meal prep you can do ahead of time to make your meals easier?

_____

_____

Cross off any meals that you do NOT need to make this week.

Meal Plan

	MON	TUES	WED	THURS	FRI	SAT	SUN
WEATHER							
BREAKFAST							
SNACK							
LUNCH							
SNACK							
DINNER (CHEDULE/THEME/ RECIPE SOURCE)							
DESSERT							

Week of _____

What's going on this week? Is there anything in your schedule that will affect what time you eat or how you prepare meals?

_____

_____

What is the weather this week? Write the forecast at the top of your Meal Plan, and make any notes here of things that might affect how you cook (using the oven, grill, etc.) or what kind of meals you want to make.

_____

_____

What theme nights do you want to include this week?

_____

_____

Is there any meal prep you can do ahead of time to make your meals easier?

_____

_____

Cross off any meals that you do NOT need to make this week.

Meal Plan

	MON	TUES	WED	THURS	FRI	SAT	SUN
WEATHER							
BREAKFAST							
SNACK							
LUNCH							
SNACK							
DINNER (CHEDULE/THEME/ RECIPE SOURCE)							
DESSERT							

Week of _____

What's going on this week? Is there anything in your schedule that will affect what time you eat or how you prepare meals?

_____

_____

What is the weather this week? Write the forecast at the top of your Meal Plan, and make any notes here of things that might affect how you cook (using the oven, grill, etc.) or what kind of meals you want to make.

_____

_____

What theme nights do you want to include this week?

_____

_____

Is there any meal prep you can do ahead of time to make your meals easier?

_____

_____

Cross off any meals that you do NOT need to make this week.

Meal Plan

	MON	TUES	WED	THURS	FRI	SAT	SUN
WEATHER							
BREAKFAST							
SNACK							
LUNCH							
SNACK							
DINNER (CHEDULE/THEME/ RECIPE SOURCE)							
DESSERT							

Week of _____

What's going on this week? Is there anything in your schedule that will affect what time you eat or how you prepare meals?

_____

_____

What is the weather this week? Write the forecast at the top of your Meal Plan, and make any notes here of things that might affect how you cook (using the oven, grill, etc.) or what kind of meals you want to make.

_____

_____

What theme nights do you want to include this week?

_____

_____

Is there any meal prep you can do ahead of time to make your meals easier?

_____

_____

Cross off any meals that you do NOT need to make this week.

Meal Plan

	MON	TUES	WED	THURS	FRI	SAT	SUN
WEATHER							
BREAKFAST							
SNACK							
LUNCH							
SNACK							
DINNER (SCHEDULE/THEME/ RECIPE SOURCE)							
DESSERT							

Week of _____

What's going on this week? Is there anything in your schedule that will affect what time you eat or how you prepare meals?

_____

_____

What is the weather this week? Write the forecast at the top of your Meal Plan, and make any notes here of things that might affect how you cook (using the oven, grill, etc.) or what kind of meals you want to make.

_____

_____

What theme nights do you want to include this week?

_____

_____

Is there any meal prep you can do ahead of time to make your meals easier?

_____

_____

Cross off any meals that you do NOT need to make this week.

Meal Plan

	MON	TUES	WED	THURS	FRI	SAT	SUN
WEATHER							
BREAKFAST							
SNACK							
LUNCH							
SNACK							
DINNER (CHEDULE/THEME/ RECIPE SOURCE)							
DESSERT							

Week of _____

What's going on this week? Is there anything in your schedule that will affect what time you eat or how you prepare meals?

_____

_____

What is the weather this week? Write the forecast at the top of your Meal Plan, and make any notes here of things that might affect how you cook (using the oven, grill, etc.) or what kind of meals you want to make.

_____

_____

What theme nights do you want to include this week?

_____

_____

Is there any meal prep you can do ahead of time to make your meals easier?

_____

_____

Cross off any meals that you do NOT need to make this week.

Meal Plan

	MON	TUES	WED	THURS	FRI	SAT	SUN
WEATHER							
BREAKFAST							
SNACK							
LUNCH							
SNACK							
DINNER (SCHEDULE/THEME/ RECIPE SOURCE)							
DESSERT							

Week of _____

What's going on this week? Is there anything in your schedule that will affect what time you eat or how you prepare meals?

_____

_____

What is the weather this week? Write the forecast at the top of your Meal Plan, and make any notes here of things that might affect how you cook (using the oven, grill, etc.) or what kind of meals you want to make.

_____

_____

What theme nights do you want to include this week?

_____

_____

Is there any meal prep you can do ahead of time to make your meals easier?

_____

_____

Cross off any meals that you do NOT need to make this week.

Meal Plan

	MON	TUES	WED	THURS	FRI	SAT	SUN
WEATHER							
BREAKFAST							
SNACK							
LUNCH							
SNACK							
DINNER (SCHEDULE/THEME/ RECIPE SOURCE)							
DESSERT							

Week of _____

What's going on this week? Is there anything in your schedule that will affect what time you eat or how you prepare meals?

_____

_____

What is the weather this week? Write the forecast at the top of your Meal Plan, and make any notes here of things that might affect how you cook (using the oven, grill, etc.) or what kind of meals you want to make.

_____

_____

What theme nights do you want to include this week?

_____

_____

Is there any meal prep you can do ahead of time to make your meals easier?

_____

_____

Cross off any meals that you do NOT need to make this week.

Meal Plan

	MON	TUES	WED	THURS	FRI	SAT	SUN
WEATHER							
BREAKFAST							
SNACK							
LUNCH							
SNACK							
DINNER (SCHEDULE/THEME/ RECIPE SOURCE)							
DESSERT							

Week of _____

What's going on this week? Is there anything in your schedule that will affect what time you eat or how you prepare meals?

_____

_____

What is the weather this week? Write the forecast at the top of your Meal Plan, and make any notes here of things that might affect how you cook (using the oven, grill, etc.) or what kind of meals you want to make.

_____

_____

What theme nights do you want to include this week?

_____

_____

Is there any meal prep you can do ahead of time to make your meals easier?

_____

_____

Cross off any meals that you do NOT need to make this week.

Meal Plan

	MON	TUES	WED	THURS	FRI	SAT	SUN
WEATHER							
BREAKFAST							
SNACK							
LUNCH							
SNACK							
DINNER (SCHEDULE/THEME/ RECIPE SOURCE)							
DESSERT							

Week of _____

What's going on this week? Is there anything in your schedule that will affect what time you eat or how you prepare meals?

_____

_____

What is the weather this week? Write the forecast at the top of your Meal Plan, and make any notes here of things that might affect how you cook (using the oven, grill, etc.) or what kind of meals you want to make.

_____

_____

What theme nights do you want to include this week?

_____

_____

Is there any meal prep you can do ahead of time to make your meals easier?

_____

_____

Cross off any meals that you do NOT need to make this week.

Meal Plan

	MON	TUES	WED	THURS	FRI	SAT	SUN
WEATHER							
BREAKFAST							
SNACK							
LUNCH							
SNACK							
DINNER (SCHEDULE/THEME/ RECIPE SOURCE)							
DESSERT							

Week of _____

What's going on this week? Is there anything in your schedule that will affect what time you eat or how you prepare meals?

_____

_____

What is the weather this week? Write the forecast at the top of your Meal Plan, and make any notes here of things that might affect how you cook (using the oven, grill, etc.) or what kind of meals you want to make.

_____

_____

What theme nights do you want to include this week?

_____

_____

Is there any meal prep you can do ahead of time to make your meals easier?

_____

_____

Cross off any meals that you do NOT need to make this week.

Meal Plan

	MON	TUES	WED	THURS	FRI	SAT	SUN
WEATHER							
BREAKFAST							
SNACK							
LUNCH							
SNACK							
DINNER (CHEDULE/THEME/ RECIPE SOURCE)							
DESSERT							

Week of _____

What's going on this week? Is there anything in your schedule that will affect what time you eat or how you prepare meals?

_____

_____

What is the weather this week? Write the forecast at the top of your Meal Plan, and make any notes here of things that might affect how you cook (using the oven, grill, etc.) or what kind of meals you want to make.

_____

_____

What theme nights do you want to include this week?

_____

_____

Is there any meal prep you can do ahead of time to make your meals easier?

_____

_____

Cross off any meals that you do NOT need to make this week.

Meal Plan

	MON	TUES	WED	THURS	FRI	SAT	SUN
WEATHER							
BREAKFAST							
SNACK							
LUNCH							
SNACK							
DINNER (SCHEDULE/THEME/ RECIPE SOURCE)							
DESSERT							

Week of _____

What's going on this week? Is there anything in your schedule that will affect what time you eat or how you prepare meals?

_____

_____

What is the weather this week? Write the forecast at the top of your Meal Plan, and make any notes here of things that might affect how you cook (using the oven, grill, etc.) or what kind of meals you want to make.

_____

_____

What theme nights do you want to include this week?

_____

_____

Is there any meal prep you can do ahead of time to make your meals easier?

_____

_____

Cross off any meals that you do NOT need to make this week.

Meal Plan

	MON	TUES	WED	THURS	FRI	SAT	SUN
WEATHER							
BREAKFAST							
SNACK							
LUNCH							
SNACK							
DINNER (SCHEDULE/THEME/ RECIPE SOURCE)							
DESSERT							

Seasonal Refresh

Welcome to a new season!

With every change of season comes a change in weather, schedules, and day-to-day activity. Use these pages to reflect on and refresh your meal plan so that it continues to work for you and fit your life.

Think back over the past 3 months.

How did your meal planning fit into your life over the past few months?

_____

_____

What worked really well for you that you want to keep doing?

_____

_____

What didn't work so well that you would like to change?

_____

_____

How many meals did you plan for during each planning session? Do you want to keep that number the same or change it?

_____

_____

How often did you go grocery shopping? Do you want to keep that frequency the same or change it?

_____

_____

What are your family's favorite recipes lately? What have you been trying and loving? (Make sure these are on your Favorite Meal Rotation List.)

_____

_____

Did you discover any new cookbooks, magazines, or blogs that you love? Add these to your resources list!

_____

_____

Now think ahead to the next 3 months...

Look at Your Weekly Schedule

Think about your average weekly schedule for this season. What events do you have going on you need to remember? Think about meetings, lessons, after school activities, etc. List out what your typical schedule looks like.

day	*typical schedule*
MONDAY	
TUESDAY	
WEDNESDAY	
THURSDAY	
FRIDAY	
SATURDAY	
SUNDAY	

How is the weather changing? How will the change affect the way you want to cook and eat? (For example, in Winter you may want more soups; during Summer you may want to grill more often, etc.)

_____

_____

Is there anything new you know you want to try? A new recipe, cuisine, or ingredient? How can you add this to your plan?

_____

_____

Do you want to add or swap out any theme nights?

_____

_____

Week of _____

What's going on this week? Is there anything in your schedule that will affect what time you eat or how you prepare meals?

_____

_____

What is the weather this week? Write the forecast at the top of your Meal Plan, and make any notes here of things that might affect how you cook (using the oven, grill, etc.) or what kind of meals you want to make.

_____

_____

What theme nights do you want to include this week?

_____

_____

Is there any meal prep you can do ahead of time to make your meals easier?

_____

_____

Cross off any meals that you do NOT need to make this week.

Meal Plan

	MON	TUES	WED	THURS	FRI	SAT	SUN
WEATHER							
BREAKFAST							
SNACK							
LUNCH							
SNACK							
DINNER (SCHEDULE/THEME/ RECIPE SOURCE)							
DESSERT							

Week of _____

What's going on this week? Is there anything in your schedule that will affect what time you eat or how you prepare meals?

_____

_____

What is the weather this week? Write the forecast at the top of your Meal Plan, and make any notes here of things that might affect how you cook (using the oven, grill, etc.) or what kind of meals you want to make.

_____

_____

What theme nights do you want to include this week?

_____

_____

Is there any meal prep you can do ahead of time to make your meals easier?

_____

_____

Cross off any meals that you do NOT need to make this week.

Meal Plan

	MON	TUES	WED	THURS	FRI	SAT	SUN
WEATHER							
BREAKFAST							
SNACK							
LUNCH							
SNACK							
DINNER (SCHEDULE/THEME/ RECIPE SOURCE)							
DESSERT							

Week of _____

What's going on this week? Is there anything in your schedule that will affect what time you eat or how you prepare meals?

_____

_____

What is the weather this week? Write the forecast at the top of your Meal Plan, and make any notes here of things that might affect how you cook (using the oven, grill, etc.) or what kind of meals you want to make.

_____

_____

What theme nights do you want to include this week?

_____

_____

Is there any meal prep you can do ahead of time to make your meals easier?

_____

_____

Cross off any meals that you do NOT need to make this week.

Meal Plan

	MON	TUES	WED	THURS	FRI	SAT	SUN
WEATHER							
BREAKFAST							
SNACK							
LUNCH							
SNACK							
DINNER (SCHEDULE/THEME/ RECIPE SOURCE)							
DESSERT							

Week of _____

What's going on this week? Is there anything in your schedule that will affect what time you eat or how you prepare meals?

_____

_____

What is the weather this week? Write the forecast at the top of your Meal Plan, and make any notes here of things that might affect how you cook (using the oven, grill, etc.) or what kind of meals you want to make.

_____

_____

What theme nights do you want to include this week?

_____

_____

Is there any meal prep you can do ahead of time to make your meals easier?

_____

_____

Cross off any meals that you do NOT need to make this week.

Meal Plan

	MON	TUES	WED	THURS	FRI	SAT	SUN
WEATHER							
BREAKFAST							
SNACK							
LUNCH							
SNACK							
DINNER (SCHEDULE/THEME/ RECIPE SOURCE)							
DESSERT							

Week of _____

What's going on this week? Is there anything in your schedule that will affect what time you eat or how you prepare meals?

_____

_____

What is the weather this week? Write the forecast at the top of your Meal Plan, and make any notes here of things that might affect how you cook (using the oven, grill, etc.) or what kind of meals you want to make.

_____

_____

What theme nights do you want to include this week?

_____

_____

Is there any meal prep you can do ahead of time to make your meals easier?

_____

_____

Cross off any meals that you do NOT need to make this week.

Meal Plan

	MON	TUES	WED	THURS	FRI	SAT	SUN
WEATHER							
BREAKFAST							
SNACK							
LUNCH							
SNACK							
DINNER (SCHEDULE/THEME/ RECIPE SOURCE)							
DESSERT							

Week of _____

What's going on this week? Is there anything in your schedule that will affect what time you eat or how you prepare meals?

_____

_____

What is the weather this week? Write the forecast at the top of your Meal Plan, and make any notes here of things that might affect how you cook (using the oven, grill, etc.) or what kind of meals you want to make.

_____

_____

What theme nights do you want to include this week?

_____

_____

Is there any meal prep you can do ahead of time to make your meals easier?

_____

_____

Cross off any meals that you do NOT need to make this week.

Meal Plan

	MON	TUES	WED	THURS	FRI	SAT	SUN
WEATHER							
BREAKFAST							
SNACK							
LUNCH							
SNACK							
DINNER (SCHEDULE/THEME/ RECIPE SOURCE)							
DESSERT							

Week of _____

What's going on this week? Is there anything in your schedule that will affect what time you eat or how you prepare meals?

_____

_____

What is the weather this week? Write the forecast at the top of your Meal Plan, and make any notes here of things that might affect how you cook (using the oven, grill, etc.) or what kind of meals you want to make.

_____

_____

What theme nights do you want to include this week?

_____

_____

Is there any meal prep you can do ahead of time to make your meals easier?

_____

_____

Cross off any meals that you do NOT need to make this week.

Meal Plan

	MON	TUES	WED	THURS	FRI	SAT	SUN
WEATHER							
BREAKFAST							
SNACK							
LUNCH							
SNACK							
DINNER (SCHEDULE/THEME/ RECIPE SOURCE)							
DESSERT							

Week of _____

What's going on this week? Is there anything in your schedule that will affect what time you eat or how you prepare meals?

_____

_____

What is the weather this week? Write the forecast at the top of your Meal Plan, and make any notes here of things that might affect how you cook (using the oven, grill, etc.) or what kind of meals you want to make.

_____

_____

What theme nights do you want to include this week?

_____

_____

Is there any meal prep you can do ahead of time to make your meals easier?

_____

_____

Cross off any meals that you do NOT need to make this week.

Meal Plan

	MON	TUES	WED	THURS	FRI	SAT	SUN
WEATHER							
BREAKFAST							
SNACK							
LUNCH							
SNACK							
DINNER (CHEDULE/THEME/ RECIPE SOURCE)							
DESSERT							

Week of _____

What's going on this week? Is there anything in your schedule that will affect what time you eat or how you prepare meals?

_____

_____

What is the weather this week? Write the forecast at the top of your Meal Plan, and make any notes here of things that might affect how you cook (using the oven, grill, etc.) or what kind of meals you want to make.

_____

_____

What theme nights do you want to include this week?

_____

_____

Is there any meal prep you can do ahead of time to make your meals easier?

_____

_____

Cross off any meals that you do NOT need to make this week.

Meal Plan

	MON	TUES	WED	THURS	FRI	SAT	SUN
WEATHER							
BREAKFAST							
SNACK							
LUNCH							
SNACK							
DINNER (SCHEDULE/THEME/ RECIPE SOURCE)							
DESSERT							

Week of _____

What's going on this week? Is there anything in your schedule that will affect what time you eat or how you prepare meals?

_____

_____

What is the weather this week? Write the forecast at the top of your Meal Plan, and make any notes here of things that might affect how you cook (using the oven, grill, etc.) or what kind of meals you want to make.

_____

_____

What theme nights do you want to include this week?

_____

_____

Is there any meal prep you can do ahead of time to make your meals easier?

_____

_____

Cross off any meals that you do NOT need to make this week.

Meal Plan

	MON	TUES	WED	THURS	FRI	SAT	SUN
WEATHER							
BREAKFAST							
SNACK							
LUNCH							
SNACK							
DINNER (SCHEDULE/THEME/ RECIPE SOURCE)							
DESSERT							

Week of _____

What's going on this week? Is there anything in your schedule that will affect what time you eat or how you prepare meals?

_____

_____

What is the weather this week? Write the forecast at the top of your Meal Plan, and make any notes here of things that might affect how you cook (using the oven, grill, etc.) or what kind of meals you want to make.

_____

_____

What theme nights do you want to include this week?

_____

_____

Is there any meal prep you can do ahead of time to make your meals easier?

_____

_____

Cross off any meals that you do NOT need to make this week.

Meal Plan

	MON	TUES	WED	THURS	FRI	SAT	SUN
WEATHER							
BREAKFAST							
SNACK							
LUNCH							
SNACK							
DINNER (SCHEDULE/THEME/ RECIPE SOURCE)							
DESSERT							

Week of _____

What's going on this week? Is there anything in your schedule that will affect what time you eat or how you prepare meals?

_____

_____

What is the weather this week? Write the forecast at the top of your Meal Plan, and make any notes here of things that might affect how you cook (using the oven, grill, etc.) or what kind of meals you want to make.

_____

_____

What theme nights do you want to include this week?

_____

_____

Is there any meal prep you can do ahead of time to make your meals easier?

_____

_____

Cross off any meals that you do NOT need to make this week.

Meal Plan

	MON	TUES	WED	THURS	FRI	SAT	SUN
WEATHER							
BREAKFAST							
SNACK							
LUNCH							
SNACK							
DINNER (CHEDULE/THEME/ RECIPE SOURCE)							
DESSERT							

Week of _____

What's going on this week? Is there anything in your schedule that will affect what time you eat or how you prepare meals?

_____

_____

What is the weather this week? Write the forecast at the top of your Meal Plan, and make any notes here of things that might affect how you cook (using the oven, grill, etc.) or what kind of meals you want to make.

_____

_____

What theme nights do you want to include this week?

_____

_____

Is there any meal prep you can do ahead of time to make your meals easier?

_____

_____

Cross off any meals that you do NOT need to make this week.

Meal Plan

	MON	TUES	WED	THURS	FRI	SAT	SUN
WEATHER							
BREAKFAST							
SNACK							
LUNCH							
SNACK							
DINNER (SCHEDULE/THEME/ RECIPE SOURCE)							
DESSERT							

Seasonal Reflection

Welcome to a new season!

With every change of season comes a change in weather, schedules, and day-to-day activity. Use these pages to reflect on and refresh your meal plan so that it continues to work for you and fit your life.

Think back over the past 3 months.

How did your meal planning fit into your life over the past few months?

_____

_____

What worked really well for you that you want to keep doing?

_____

_____

What didn't work so well that you would like to change?

_____

_____

How many meals did you plan for during each planning session? Do you want to keep that number the same or change it?

_____

_____

How often did you go grocery shopping? Do you want to keep that frequency the same or change it?

_____

_____

What are your family's favorite recipes lately? What have you been trying and loving? (Make sure these are on your Favorite Meal Rotation List.)

_____

_____

Did you discover any new cookbooks, magazines, or blogs that you love? Add these to your resources list!

_____

_____

Congratulations on completing an entire year of meal planning!

I hope this has helped you on your meal planning journey.

Come visit me at **www.thegingeredwhisk.com** for recipe inspiration
and to order your new meal planner book to guide you through
another year of adventures in meal planning!

Made in the USA
Coppell, TX
28 February 2023

13577251R00090